ST. PATRICK'S DAY
IRISH TRADITIONS
+ HISTORY

FOR CHILDREN AGE 2-6

MORE KIDS BOOKS!

Farting books for kids

Luke the Leprechaun Can't Stop Farting
Louie the Leprechaun Farts for Ireland
Leo the Leprechaun's Farting Dilemma

Unicorn books for kids

My sister is a unicorn series
Ciara & the Unicorn's New York Adventure
Ciara & the Unicorn's Farm Fiasco
Ciara & the Unicorn's Cake Shop Surprise
Ciara & the Unicorn's Save Valentine's Day

FOR EVERY WONDERFUL CHILD WHO LOVES ALL THINGS IRISH...

THIS BOOK BELONGS TO:

St. Patrick's Day is famous in Ireland and throughout the WORLD!

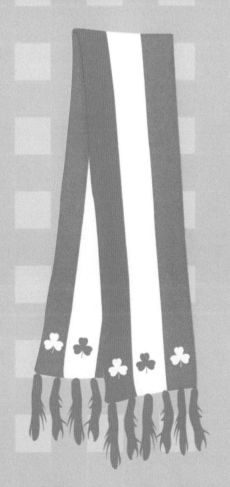

It's a very special day on March 17 every year, when everything goes GREEN and we have a big party!

Did you know? A leprechaun is a small magical person who is from Ireland.

GOOD LUCK!

On St. Patrick's Day go for a leprechaun hunt. Go outside and listen carefully for the 'tap-tap-tap' of the leprechauns making shoes and follow the noise.

Look for a rainbow. At the end of each rainbow is a pot of gold belonging to a leprechaun!

Don't forget to decorate your house with green, white and gold decorations!

DID YOU KNOW:

Green, white & gold is the colour of the Irish flag.

Geography Test

Find Ireland on a map of the world.

Make St. Patrick's Day Cards for your family and friends.

All you need is some paper, some green pencils and your imagination!

Irish music is famous around the world. Listen to or try your hand at playing the fiddle (violin), harp, bodhran (type of drum) or tin whistle.

A Ceili is a type of Irish party that usually includes lots of music and dancing. They are a LOT of fun!

Dress up in Irish costumes and have your own St. Patrick's Day parade.

Irish people love parties and parades, especially with a traditional Irish band playing!

Make some delicious Irish food like corned beef and cabbage, shepherd's pie and Irish soda bread.

Irish soda bread

Cabbage

Corned beef

Where did the name St. Patrick come from?

Patrick was a man who lived with his family in Wales. One night, there was an attack from a group of Irish men who had travelled across the Irish sea. They captured Patrick and brought him back to Ireland as a slave.

Patrick spent six years as a slave in Ireland. He was a shepherd and took care of sheep on the mountains in Ireland.

After six years, Patrick escaped. He travelled to the sea, took a trip on a boat going to Great Britain and returned to his family.

One night back at home, he had a dream about returning to Ireland.

He woke up and decided to become a priest and then return to Ireland and convert the Irish people to Christianity.

After many years of study, he became a priest, returned to Ireland and spent many years there spreading Christianity.

St. Patrick is now the Patron Saint of Ireland.

And we celebrate him each year
on March 17, St. Patrick's Day.
There are also many unusual
legends about St. Patrick!

Legend has it that St. Patrick banished all the snakes from Ireland.

One day, St. Patrick left his walking stick on the ground while he talked. He talked for so long that day, that his walking stick started to grow into a tree!

St. Patricks explained the idea of the Holy Trinity, by comparing it to a shamrock with three leaves. Shamrocks are now famous in Ireland.

Patrick converted the King of Munster to Christianity in Tipperary. By accident, he pushed a huge spear through the Kings foot. The King thought it was part of the ceremony (phew).

CONGRATULATIONS!

YOU FINISHED THIS BOOK. IF YOU ENJOYED
THIS BOOK PLEASE LEAVE A REVIEW!

EASTER TRADITIONS AND HISTORY
FOR CHILDREN AGE 2-6
MATILDA WALSH

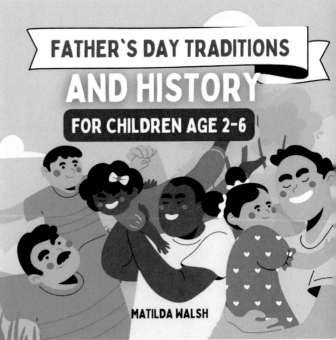

FATHER'S DAY TRADITIONS AND HISTORY
FOR CHILDREN AGE 2-6
MATILDA WALSH

KIDS BOOKS

ENJOY THE FUNNY UNICORN BOOK SERIES!

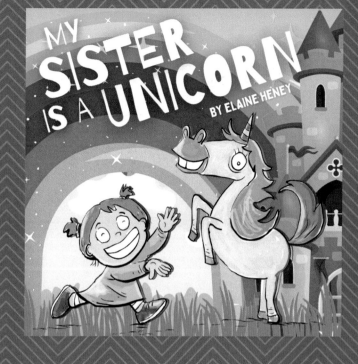

MY SISTER IS A UNICORN
BY ELAINE HENEY

CIARA AND THE UNICORN SAVE VALENTINE'S DAY
BY ELAINE HENEY

CIARA AND THE UNICORN'S CAKE SHOP SURPRISE
BY ELAINE HENEY

LOVE FARTS?

ENJOY THE FUNNY FARTING BOOKS!

BILLY THE BUNNY AND THE EASTER FARTS

MATILDA WALSH

LOUIE THE LEPRECHAUN FARTS FOR IRELAND

MATILDA WALSH

LUKE THE LEPRECHAUN CAN'T STOP FARTING

MATILDA WALSH